Spider

Karen Hartley,
Chris Macro,
and Philip Taylor

Heinemann Library
Chicago, Illinois

Text and cover designed by Celia Floyd
Printed and bound in Hong Kong, China, by South China Printing Co. Ltd.

05 04 03 02 01
10 9 8 7 6 5 4 3 2 1

Library of Congress Cataloging-in-Publication Data
Hartley, Karen, 1949-
    Spider / Karen Hartley, Chris Macro, and Philip Taylor.
            p. cm. – (Bug books)
        Includes bibliographical references and index.
        Summary: A simple introduction to the physical characteristics,
    diet, life cycle, predators, habitat, and lifespan of spiders.
        ISBN 1-57572-799-4 (lib. bdg.) ISBN 1-58810-322-6 (pbk. bdg.)
        1. Spiders—Juvenile literature. [1. Spiders.] I. Macro,
    Chris, 1940- . II. Taylor, Philip, 1949- . III. Title.
    IV. Series.
    QL458.4.H37   1999
    595.4'4—dc21   98-42673
                                                              CIP
                                                              AC

Acknowledgments
The Publishers would like to thank the following for permission to reproduce photographs:
Ardea/T. Bomford, p. 29; J. Clegg, p. 11; B. Gibbons, pp. 4, 12, 18; A. Warren, pp. 7, 9; A. Weaving, p. 27; W. Weisser, p. 5; Bruce Coleman Ltd./J. Burton, p. 14; Jurka, p. 21; Dr. F. Sauer, pp. 6, 20; A. Stillwell, p. 28; Garden and Wildlife Matters/S. Apps, p. 15; M. Collins, p. 17; NHPA/S. Dalton, p. 22; Okapia/H. Reinhard, p. 24; Oxford Scientific Films/K. Atkinson, p. 25; M. Black, p. 10; N. Bromhall, p. 8; J. Cooke, p. 19; M. Fogden, pp. 16, 23; M. Leach, p. 26; S. Morris, p. 13.

Cover photos: Gareth Boden (child); NHPA/S. Dalton (spider).
Illustration: Pennant Illustration/ Alan Fraser, p. 30.

Every effort has been made to contact copyright holders of any material reproduced in this book. Any omissions will be rectified in subsequent printings if notice is given to the publisher.

Some words are shown in bold, **like this**. You can find out what they mean by looking in the glossary.

Contents

What Are Spiders?

Spiders are small animals. They have eight legs. Spiders spin silk. Most spiders make **webs** out of silk. **Insects** get stuck in the sticky web. Spiders eat them.

Some spiders make a thin line of silk to trap insects. Their food comes to them. Other spiders hunt for their food. There are over 30 thousand kinds of spiders.

What Spiders Look Like

Spiders can be short and fat. They can be long and thin. They have no bones. Their skin is hard. Many have eight eyes. Some only have two.

Most spiders are brown, gray, or black. Some are as colorful as butterflies. This crab spider can change colors. It goes from white to yellow. It hides in flowers.

How Big Are Spiders?

The **male** spider is smaller than the **female** spider. Some spiders are smaller than the head of a pin.

Spiders that live in hot places can grow bigger than your hand. Some spiders are big enough to eat birds and frogs.

How Spiders Are Born

The **male** spider has to get the **female** spider to see him. Some males tap on her **web.** Some wave their legs. After they **mate,** the female lays eggs.

Some spiders wait weeks or months to lay their eggs. Many make **egg sacs** to hold them. Some stay with the sacs. Others leave. Some carry them around.

How Spiders Grow

Baby spiders look like their parents. But they are tiny. **Spiderlings** are born blind. Their bodies are light yellow. They stay in the **egg sac** until it is warm.

Spiders **molt** as they grow. Their old skin drops off. Most spiders molt five to nine times before they grow up. Tarantulas molt 20 times.

What Spiders Eat

Some spiders eat flies and other **insects.**
Many spiders catch flies in their **webs.**
All spiders have **fangs**. They use their
fangs and **poison glands** to kill insects.

The poison also makes the insects softer and easier to eat. Spiders can't chew. They suck up their food. Some very big spiders eat lizards, birds, and frogs.

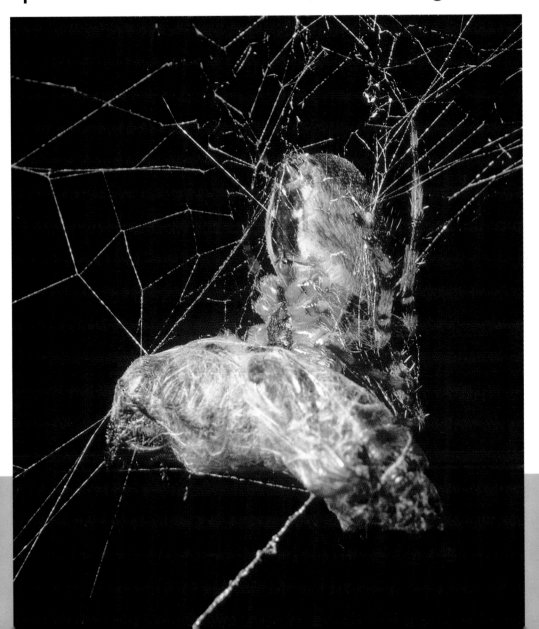

Which Animals Eat Spiders?

Wasps eat spiders. Hunting wasps jump on spiders from behind. Then they carry them to a tunnel in the ground. The spiders cannot move. The wasps eat them alive.

Spiders eat other spiders. Pirate spiders eat only other kinds of spiders. Birds, snakes, frogs, toads, lizards, and some **insects** eat spiders, too.

Where Spiders Live

Spiders live where they can find food. You will find spiders in parks, woods, and gardens. You will even find them in your house. Some live in holes between rocks. Others live in leaves where it is dark and **damp.**

Some tiny spiders live in the fur of big animals. In hot places, some spiders live in holes in the ground. Spiders live in caves, swamps, and deserts.

How Spiders Move

Spiders walk on eight legs. They move two legs at a time. Some spiders can move as fast as people. Spiders can also walk on walls and ceilings.

Spiders have special pads on their feet.
The pads are oily. They stop the spiders
from sticking to their **webs.** Crab spiders
can walk sideways and backwards.

How Long Spiders Live

Most spiders live for about a year.
Many spiders die when they are babies.
Sometimes the **female** spider dies after
she lays her eggs.

Tarantulas are the biggest spiders in the world. They live in warm places. Pet tarantulas can live for twenty years.

What Spiders Do

All spiders look for food. Some spiders build **webs.** A spider builds its web early in the morning. It takes about an hour. Now it can rest in a quiet, dark place.

The funnel-web spider lives in its web. It spins a big web in grass or under rocks and logs. It hides inside its web. When food comes, it runs out and jumps on it.

How Are Spiders Special?

Spiders have special hairs on their legs. The hairs move if an **insect** lands on the **web.** This tells them that food is here.

Spiders are also special because they can make silk. They spin silk from their **spinnerets**. Spiders use their spinnerets like fingers. Spinnerets can stretch out or pull back. They can even squeeze.

Thinking About Spiders

This spider hides in flowers. It can change its colors. Why does it do that?

Do you know the name of this spider?

What do you think this spider eats?

How long do you think it has taken the spider to make this **web?**

How do you think the web helps the spider?

Bug Map

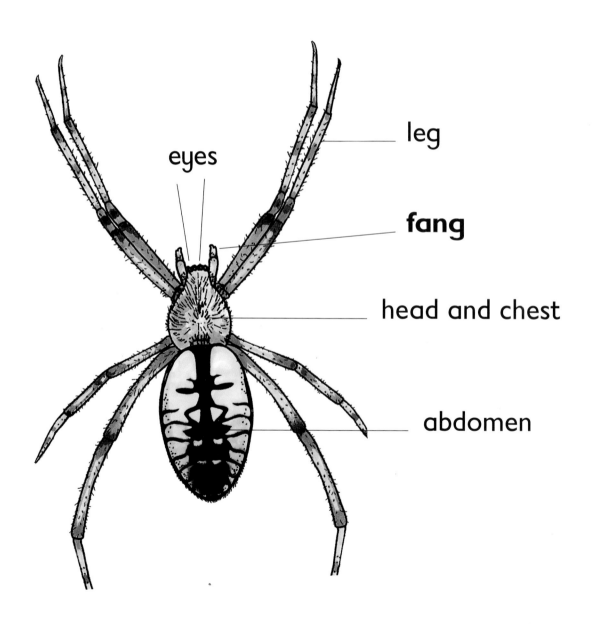

eyes

leg

fang

head and chest

abdomen

Glossary

damp little bit wet

egg sac silk bag that the female makes to hold the eggs

fang claw on a spider's head; some give out poison

female woman or girl

insect small animal with six legs, a body that has three parts, and usually having wings

male man or boy

mate to join with another to make babies

molt to shed skin

poison gland body part that makes poison

spiderling baby spider

spinneret finger-like part under the back of the spider's body, used to make silk

web pattern made from sticky threads of silk, used to catch food

More Books to Read

Fowler, Allan. *Spiders Are Not Insects*. Danbury, Conn.: Children's Press, 1996.

Gibbons, Gail. *Spiders*. New York: Holiday House, 1993.

Glaser, Linda. *Spectacular Spiders*. Brookfield, Conn.: Millbrook Press, 1998.

Index